CLASSIFICATION

by
J. McRee Elrod
Second Edition

Modern Library Practices Series, No. 3

The Scarecrow Press, Inc.
Metuchen, N.J. & London
1978

First edition published, 1969, by Educational Methods, Inc.

Library of Congress Cataloging in Publication Data

Elrod, J   McRee.
    Classification.

    (His Modern library practices series ; no. 3)
    1.   Classification, Dewey decimal--Programmed
instruction.   2.   Classification, Library of Congress--
Programmed instruction.   I.   Title.   II.   Series.
Z674.E47   no. 3   [Z696.D51955]   025s   [025.4]   77-17282
ISBN 0-8108-1094-8

This second printing of the second edition incorporates a number of revisions and corrections and is current as of January, 1979.

INTRODUCTION

The program should not be used as a substitute for a professional course in cataloging. It may serve, however, as a self-training program for nonprofessional library workers, or as a self-instructional adjunct in library science courses in cataloging. In either situation use of the program will reduce considerably the time that professors or catalogers must spend imparting factual and procedural information.

The program is appropriate for both students and library sub-professionals whose work requires knowledge of classification and book numbering systems.

The program contains instructional sequences for libraries using either the Dewey or the Library of Congress classifications and either Cutter or Cutter-Sanborn author marks. The table of contents following this introduction provides an overview of the entire program. Readers interested in only certain sequences may locate them easily by consulting the contents page.

Before proceeding with this program you should have the following readily available for easy reference.

1. Dewey Decimal Classification, 16th or later edition, and/or

2. The Library of Congress Classification outline and class schedules.

3. A Cutter and/or Cutter-Sanborn table.

After you have examined the table of contents, read the instructions for using the program which immediately follows the contents page.

CONTENTS

HOW TO USE THIS PROGRAM

This programed unit has been designed to help you learn the technical details of library cataloging. The information you need and the tasks you must perform to do that job well are broken down into step-by-step learning sequences called frames. At each step or numbered frame you are usually asked to answer a question or to perform a task.

Once you have responded to a frame you'll want to find out whether you were right. To help you confirm your answer without delay, the correct answers are printed just below each frame.

Always check and correct any mistakes before you go on. If you made an error be sure you know why. Avoid looking at the correct answer until after you have made your own response. If you look before answering, you will only impair your own learning.

ANSWER MASK

To help you avoid seeing the correct answers inadvertently before marking your answer, take a blank piece of 8-1/2" x 11" paper, fold it in half and use it as an answer mask in the following way.

1.. As you start each new page cover the entire page with the mask.

2. Slide the mask down until you see the horizontal line across the entire page. This line separates each frame from its correct answer.

3. When you reach the horizontal line, stop the mask. Read the frame carefully; then do what is asked. In most cases you will write something down (either in the book or on a separate piece of paper). It is very important that you follow all directions precisely.

4. Slide the mask down to reveal the correct answer. If your answer was right, slide the mask down to reveal all of the next numbered frame and proceed.

5. If your answer was wrong, go back, reread the frame (if necessary, reread several preceding frames) until you understand your own error and know why the answer given is correct. Then proceed to the next frame.

If you encounter anything you don't understand or if you need any kind of help, consult your supervisor or your instructor. Now turn to page 1 and begin.

1. Classification is defined by the <u>A.L.A. Glossary of Library Terms</u> as:

   1. "A systematic scheme for the arrangement of books and other material according to subject or form.

   2. The assigning of books to their proper places in a system of classification."

   There are many systems of classification. The two in most common use are the <u>Dewey Decimal Classification</u> (DC) and the <u>Library of Congress Classification</u> (LC). This program will be concerned with how books and other library materials are given numbers which place them in their proper places in either of these two systems.

   If you are using this program as an introduction to classification you may wish to use all of its frames. If you are already working in a library, however, you may wish to take only those frames which apply to your situation.

   Each book in a library has been assigned a call number. This call number appears not only on the book; it also appears on the catalog card that has been prepared for the book.

   a. On the book the call numbers appear where? _____
      _____

   b. Where do they appear on the catalog card? _____
      _____

---

a. lower spine; The word "spine" is used rather than the word "back" since "back" might be misunderstood to mean back cover.

b. upper left corner

2. The call number serves several purposes:

   a. it gives order to the arrangement of books on the shelf,

b. it provides a symbol for locating, lending and re-
placing books.

Each call number should be unique; no two books may be
assigned the same call number.

What do you think the result would be if more than one
book were assigned the same call number? _____

_____

It would lead to confusion in arranging and locating books by
their call numbers (or any similar answer)

3. The call number consists of two main parts:

1. The first part is called the <u>classification</u> number or
    class number.

    It is usually based on the subject of the book. In
    literature it is usually based on the form of the
    book, e.g., poetry, drama, fiction, etc.

    A typical call number appears below labeled as to
    first part and second part.

    first part   327.73072
    second part   D18s

    327.73072 is called the _____ or the
    _____ number.

    It is based on the _____

_____

classification or class
subject of the book

4. The second part of the call number is usually based on
    the author of the book, and is called the <u>book</u> number.

    For biography and literary criticism it is usually based
    on subject.

In the frame above, D18 is based on the _____ of the book and is called the _____ number.

---

author
book

5. Additional parts of the call number may be based on title, edition, date of publication, volume, language or translator. For example, a small letter can be used to indicate title.

   Below is the second part of a call number, the book number. Circle and label the author symbol and the title letter.

   D18s

(D18) (S)←———— title letter
   ＼———— author symbol

6. The classification number is chosen from the classification schedules or tables used by the library. These tables of numbers or letters-and-numbers provide for the orderly arrangement of all subjects in the library collection.

   The number may also come from some other source, such as a printed catalog card, which is then checked against the library's classification practice.

   The classification number is also called the _____ number. The classification number and the book number combined are called the _____ number.

---

class
call

7. In library cataloging practice the word "class" is also used as a verb; it means "to classify" or to assign the _____ number.

---

class or classification

8. Several principles have come to be accepted by classifiers. These principles help in selecting the correct classification number in cases where doubt exists.

   Principle 1: Except for literature, class first by subject and then by form.

   A dictionary (form) of mathematical (subject) terms would class in the number for: (circle one)

       a. dictionaries
       b. mathematics

---

mathematics (subject first--then form)

9. Classification schedules have form numbers to add to the subject numbers to divide the dictionaries and histories and other special forms from books which treat the subject generally.

   A history of science would class in the number for _____.

   Added to this number would be a _____ number to indicate that the form of the book is a _____.

---

science
form; history

-4-

10. <u>Principle 2</u>: In literature, class first by the language originally used by the author,

then by the <u>form</u> (poetry, drama, fiction, etc.) in some classifications,

and/or then by <u>period</u> (when the author wrote)

according to the provisions of your schedules.

The example below, a D.C. (Dewey Decimal Classification) number, is the call number for Goethe's Faust written in the original language (German) and published in 1965.

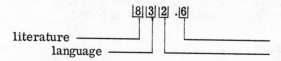

German literature is classed in the number 830. Label the other parts of the number above.

The 2 represents the <u>form</u> of German literature (drama)
The 6 represents the <u>period</u> (date) during which the work was written

11. Some books contain two subjects. Sometimes one of the two subjects is treated more fully than the other, that is, it has more pages devoted to it.

<u>Principle 3</u>: Books which treat two subjects should be classed in the <u>first subject treated</u> unless a greater number of pages is given to the other subject.

An introduction to algebra and trigonometry (in that order) with an equal number of pages given to each would receive the number for _____.

---

algebra

12. Under which respective subject would you classify the following books whose titles are

    a) Birds and Wildlife of the Amazon (This book deals mostly with the wildlife of that region) _____

    b) Language and Information (Both topics are treated in approximately the same number of pages)_____

    c) Knitting and Crocheting for Beginners (The main portion of this book is devoted to learning to knit) _____

    d) Beautify Your Home: the Homemaker's Guide to Interior Decorating and Landscape Design (Interior design is dealt with in pages 3-196, landscape design is discussed in pages 197-250) _____

---

a. wildlife
b. language
c. knitting
d. interior decorating

13. Some classifiers class books treating two subjects equally in the first of those two subjects in the classification tables rather than the first to be treated in the book.

By this method all books treating those two subjects together would be in the same class number regardless of which of the two subjects is treated first in the individual book.

    Principle 4: Books which treat three or more subjects are classed in the more general subject of which all three are a part.

               An introduction to algebra, trigonometry, and geometry would class in the number for _____.

---

mathematics

14. Some classifiers make the break between three and four subjects--classing books treating three subjects in the first subject treated.

Books treating four subjects or more are classed in the larger subject.

There is a general class for books which treat a group of subjects for which there is no larger subject.

Under which subject would you classify the following titles:

a) A Handbook on the Care and Feeding of Dogs, Cats, Canaries and Hamsters. _____

b) An Introduction to Judaism, Christianity, Buddhism and Taoism. _____

c) Apples, Oranges, Pears and Plums. _____

---

a) pets or animals
b) religion
c) fruits

15. Principle 5: Books which treat three or more subjects which have no larger subject; e.g., philosophy, religion, science, and history; are classed in the _____ class.

---

general

16. Principle 6: If one subject modifies another subject, class in the subject modified. Pressurization of aircraft would class in aircraft, not air pressure.

Decoration in architecture would class in _____.

---

architecture

-7-

17.   Principle 7:   If the choice is between subject and place, class by subject.

Thus, Chinese religion would class in _____.

---

religion

18.   The sciences in Great Britain would class in _____.

---

science

19.   Principle 8:   If the choice is between further division by subject or division by place, prefer further division by subject.

Indicate in words, the order in which the following titles would be classed:

a)   Computer-aided teaching in the United States ____

b)   Taxation of land property in France _____

---

a)   Teaching--computer aided--United States
b)   Land property--taxes--France

Classification tables have numbers for geographic subdivision of subjects.

20.   Principle 9:   In public libraries class biography as an independent class; fiction may be un-classified.

In academic libraries class biographies with the subject or country with which the person was concerned.

Only individuals not connected with the history of any country or any subject area and collective biography too general to be classified with a subject would be placed in the biography number.

a. In a public library a life of Beethoven could class in _____.

b. In a university library a life of Beethoven should class in _____.

---

a. biography
b. music

21. <u>Principle 10</u>: Sometimes, in borderline cases, you must consider the purpose of the author in writing or the use which will be made of a book in your collection in selecting a number.

These factors may be particularly important in determining whether a particular book belongs in the pure or applied sciences (science or technology).

Under which subjects would you classify the following books?

a) <u>Transportation in a past age</u> (This book describes the role played by the horse before the advent of the automobile)

   _____

b) <u>Music in my toes</u> (This is an autobiography of the dancer Fred Astaire) [for use in an academic library]

   _____

c) <u>Water into gold</u> (In his preface, the author of this book states that his purpose is to illustrate what can be done to arid country by the process of irrigation)

   _____

a) Horses
b) Dancing
c) Irrigation

22. Now, let's review the ten principles we've covered.
Read each carefully and fill in the missing information.

> Principle 1:   Except for literature, class first by
> _____, then by _____.

---

subject; form

23. Principle 2:   In literature, class first by the _____
originally used by the author, then by
_____, and/or then by _____.

---

language; form; period

24. Principle 3:   Books which treat two subjects equally
should be classed in _____.

---

the first subject treated

25. Books which treat one subject more completely than
the other should be classed in _____.

---

the subject treated more completely

26. In classifying books that treat two subjects equally
some classifiers class such books in the _____
_____.

---

first of the two subjects appearing in the classification table

27. <u>Principle 4</u>: Books that treat three or more subjects are classed in _____.

---

the more general subject of which all are a part

28. Some classifiers make the break between three and four subjects.

Books that treat three subjects are classed in _____ _____.

---

the first subject treated

29. Books that treat four subjects are classed in _____ _____.

---

the larger subject

30. <u>Principle 5</u>: Books which treat three or more subjects which have no larger subjects are classed in the _____ class.

---

general

31. <u>Principle 6</u>: If one subject modifies another, class in the _____.

---

subject modified

32. <u>Principle 7</u>: If the choice is between subject and place, class by _____.

---

subject

33. Principle 8: If the choice is between further division by subject or division by place, divide further by _____.

_____

subject

34. Principle 9: In public libraries class biography as _____.

In academic libraries class biography by _____.

_____

an independent class (biography)
subject or country

35. Principle 10: Sometimes, in borderline cases, it is necessary to classify a book properly to consider the _____ of the author and/ or the _____.

_____

purpose
use which will be made of the book in your collection

36. Classification tables divide subjects into main classes. Science is a main class.

Classes are then divided into divisions. Mathematics is a division of science.

Divisions have sections. Algebra is a section of mathematics.

Sections have subsections to any degree. Theory of numbers is a subsection of algebra.

Sections and subsections are sometimes called subdivisions.

Following are two illustrations of this kind of division taken from two classification tables which will be described in greater detail later in the program. Examine them carefully.

[DC]	[LC]	
500	Q	Science (class)
510	QA	Mathematics (division)
512	QA150-290	Algebra (section)
512.7	QA240	Theory of numbers (sub-section)

[DC]	[LC]	
300	H	Social sciences
330	HB-HJ	Economics
336	HJ	Public finance
336.2	HJ2240-7395	Taxation

---

37. Taxation is a _____ of public finance.

---

subsection

38. Public finance is a _____ of economics.

---

section

39. Economics is a _____ of the _____ social sciences.

---

division; class

40. The examples were drawn from the two most commonly used classification systems--Dewey Decimal Classification (DC) and Library of Congress Classification (LC).

From the examples you can tell that the system that uses only numbers is _____ .

The system that uses both letters and numbers is

_____ .

DC; LC

41. In DC the hundreds are always <u>classes</u>.

    The tens are _____ .

    The digits are _____ .

    The digits to the right of the decimal are _____ .

---

divisions
sections
subsections (Following a decimal, subsections may be carried to any number of decimal places.)

42. LC is irregular. The number of letters or numbers designating a class, division or section are determined by the amount of publication in that subject at the time the schedule was created.

    Check the illustrations in frame 36 and notice that the division Mathematics was assigned only the letters

    _____ .

    On the other hand, economics, which is also a _____ has been assigned _____ through _____ .

QA; division, HB through HJ

43. If you are interested only in LC or a similar mixed notation system (e.g., Cutter's Expansive classification) skip to frame 83.

-14-

If you are using some system other than LC such as Cutter's Expansive, the principles given will apply but the sample numbers will not.

If you are interested in DC or other similar decimal notation systems (e.g., Universal Decimal Classification in Europe; Nippon Decimal Classification and Korean Decimal Classification in Asia) continue with the next frame.

If you are using UDC, NDC, or KDC the principles given will apply but the sample numbers will not.

You already know that DC is divided into _____ main classes.

---

ten

45. You should memorize these (or the ten classes of the decimal system you are using). Read the following list a few times and then proceed to the next frame.

000	Generalities
100	Philosophy and related disciplines including psychology
200	Religion
300	Social sciences
400	Languages
500	Pure sciences
600	Technology (Applied Sciences)
700	The Arts including music and recreation
800	Literature and rhetoric
900	History and related disciplines including geography and biography

---

Go on to the next frame.

46. Now complete the missing classes.

```
000   _____
100   Philosophy and related disciplines including
        psychology
200   _____
300   Social sciences
400   _____
500   Pure sciences
600   _____
700   The Arts including music and recreation
800   _____
900   History and related disciplines including geogra-
        phy and biography
```

```
000   Generalities
200   Religion
400   Language
600   Technology (Applied Sciences)
800   Literature and Rhetoric
```

47. Now complete the list.

```
000   _____
100   _____
200   _____
300   _____
400   _____
500   _____
600   _____
700   _____
800   _____
900   _____
```

Check your responses with the list in frame 45.

48.　Fill in the class numbers of each of the classes below:

Language　　　　　　　　　　　　　　＿＿＿＿＿
Arts, music and recreation　　　　　＿＿＿＿＿
Philosophy, psychology　　　　　　　＿＿＿＿＿
Social Science　　　　　　　　　　　＿＿＿＿＿
History, geography, biography　　　　＿＿＿＿＿
Generalities　　　　　　　　　　　　＿＿＿＿＿
Religion　　　　　　　　　　　　　　＿＿＿＿＿
Pure Sciences　　　　　　　　　　　＿＿＿＿＿
Technology　　　　　　　　　　　　＿＿＿＿＿
Literature and Rhetoric　　　　　　　＿＿＿＿＿

Language	400
Arts	700
Philosophy	100
Social Science	300
History	900
Generalities	000
Religion	200
Pure Science	500
Technology	600
Literature	800

49.　When you have mastered the classes you should memorize some of the divisions. Which ones will depend
upon the emphasis of your library, but the following
are usually helpful.

150	Psychology		780	Music
220	Bible		790	Recreation
320	Political science		910	Geography
330	Economics		920	Biography
370	Education		940	Europe
510	Mathematics		950	Asia
530	Physics			
540	Chemistry			and the following sections:
			971	Canada
			973	U.S.

Don't let this overwhelm you. They will come with
use.

Go on to the next frame.

50. DC has gone through many editions. An abridged edition and a standard edition are usually kept in print.

When the 17th edition appeared in 1965, work had already begun on the 18th edition. The abridged edition is one volume. The 16th and 17th standard editions are two volumes with index and auxiliary tables in the second volume; the 18th ed. is three volumes: tables, schedules, and index.

DC is very regular and often repeats numbers with the same meaning. Thus when you know that 420 is English language you can quickly learn that 192 is English philosophy, 759.2 is English painting, 820 is English literature, and 942 is English history. (But the 19th ed. of DC will revise 941-942.)

If 430 is German language, what is 830? _____

943? _____

------

830 - German literature
943 - German history

51. If 944 is French history, what is 440? _____

French language

52. You should not expect to memorize complete tables. There is an index to help you locate numbers. You will greatly speed your use of the classification, however, if you are familiar with some of the most frequently used numbers and with the structure of the classification as a whole.

Never assign a number from memory or from the index without consulting the tables.

Examine the two volumes of the 16th or 17th or 18th edition of DC. Note the location of the summary, the index, and the table of form divisions (16th), standard subdivisions and area table (17th), or tables (18th).

For the remainder of the program consult the index or tables whenever they will help you in answering a frame.

DC provides a table of standard subdivisions (formerly form divisions) which can be applied many places in the tables.

In the most recent editions of DC these have been further divided themselves. The most commonly used ones follow. These, like the main classes, should be memorized.

-01 Philosophy of
-03 Dictionary, encyclopedia or concordance
-05 Serial of
-06 Organization or society of
-07 Study and teaching of
-08 Collection or anthology of
-09 History or local (geographical) treatment of

Unless otherwise directed in the tables, standard subdivisions are always preceded by only one zero. Thus a dictionary of science would be _____ .

---

503 (Remember pure science is class 500. Dictionary in the list above is -03.)

53. In the 16th and 18th editions of DC a dictionary of mathematics would be assigned what number? _____

In the 17th edition this was changed to what number?

_____

510.3
510.03

54. The 510 Mathematics schedule in the 18th ed. is new. Whether to reclassify to conform to new editions of DC is a decision which must be made locally.

Many numbers remain the same. In any edition a history of algebra is _____ .

---

512. 09

55. A history of the theory of numbers would be _____
in the 18th ed. , but _____ in the 17th.

---

512. 709 [18th ed.]
512. 8109 [17th ed.]

56. DC also provides for geographical subdivision. Through the 16th ed. this was done in two ways.

At some numbers the direction would be to divide like the 900's. Thus 73 from 973 (U. S. history) would be added to 327 (foreign relations) to give U. S. foreign relations.

At any other number the form number 09 could be used divided like the 900's. Thus 330. 973 would be the economic history or conditions of the U. S.

In 18th ed. DC an areas table is provided. The number from this areas table is added to 09 or to numbers in the table as directed.

Find and examine the areas table in 18th ed. , volume one.

The area number for France is -44.

The geography of France is 914. 4; the foreign relations of France is 327. 44; the foreign relations of the U. S. with France is 327. 73044; and the economic conditions in France is 330. 944.

In each case the area number -44 was added as directed in the tables.

Using the 18th edition of the Dewey Decimal Classification (DC) assign class numbers to the following titles.

a) Elementary education in Japan _____

b) The distribution of minerals in Australia _____

c) Modern Encyclopedia of Applied Science and Technology _____

d) The Birds of Southern California _____

---

a) 372.952
b) 549.994
c) 603
d) 598.297949

57. When you wish to divide a number geographically and there is no such direction--use 09 and the area number (in 16th ed. 09 divided like history).

Assign class numbers to the following titles.

a) The Volcanoes of Hawaii _____

b) Medical practices in Great Britain _____

c) Cattle ranching in Argentina _____

d) Mountain railway systems in Siberia _____

---

a) 551.2109969
b) 610.942
c) 636.2010982
d) 385.60957

58. When there is no number for a specific subject you wish to class, use the number for the larger subject of which it is a part. Do not make up additional subdivisions--they will conflict with future DC expansions.

Assign class numbers to the following titles:

a) A textbook of dental nursing _____

b) The effect of random deletion of terms in index-
   ing _____

c) Computational linguistics _____

d) A survey of mechanized library circulation systems _____

---

a) 617.6023
b) 029.5
c) 415
d) 025.6

59. DC numbers appear at the bottom of many LC printed
    cards, and commercial cards may be purchased with
    the numbers printed in call number position. Such num-
    bers must be checked against the library's shelf list to
    determine if they conform to local classification prac-
    tice.

    In the 16th ed. and on LC cards 1952-1958, 14th ed.
    numbers are indicated by a dagger and 15th ed. num-
    bers by an asterisk where the editions differ.

    From 1965 to 1970, 17th ed. numbers appeared on LC
    cards.

    Earlier edition numbers are indicated in the 17th ed.
    by square brackets.

    For more on printed cards see Choice of Main and
    Added Entries, another program in the Modern Library
    Practices Series.

Go on to the next frame.

60. In selecting a number, care must be taken to see that it falls within the proper division and class. Would a map receive the number 025.176? _____

Before deciding, remember to look at the class, division and section in which this subsection is found.

No

61. Why would a map not receive the number 025.176?

_____

The number 025.176 is the division 020 - Library Science.

62. In what number would a map be classed? _____

912

63. What would be classed in 025.176? _____ .

_____

A book about handling maps in libraries

64. It is in keeping with this principle--that books should not be classed in divisions in which they do not belong --that the 17th ed. moved cultural anthropology from 572 (biological sciences) to 390 (customs); the 18th ed. moved the subject to 301.2.

Broad classification limits the length of the number so that many books fall within one classification number.

Close classification is assigning numbers as fully as provided in the tables so that few books fall within any one number.

Many public and smaller libraries prefer broad classification. While subsections may be dropped, it is better to use all sections; if the library wishes later to class more closely subsections may be added but zeros would have to be erased before additional sections could be supplied.

Many academic and larger libraries prefer close classification.

Broad classification to just the division, however, may be used in philosophy (190), theology (230), and law (340), in order to keep together works by the same persons in these areas.

If broad classification is used in law, the section 341, international law, should still be used since books in this area are not "law books" in the usual sense of the words.

For example, an academic or larger library would classify a book on water birds at 598.2924, while a public or smaller library might prefer to class it at 598-- the general class number for reptiles and birds. Or, as another example, a book on the resurrection of Christ might be classed under 232.5 in a large library but under the broad class number 230 in a small library.

For each of the following titles assign first a broad classification number (to the section level), and then a narrow one.

a) Welfare services to the blind _____ _____

b) The Nuremberg trials: trials of war criminals

   _____ _____

c) How to play lawn tennis _____ _____

d) The treatment of the common cold _____

   _____

---

a) 362; 362.41
b) 341; 341.69
c) 796; 796.342
d) 616; 616.205

65. Assign complete class numbers to the following book titles.

a) History of Judaism
b) Koran _____
c) The Olympian gods _____
d) Stories of Christian missions in Korea _____
e) History of the YMCA in America _____
f) Christ and society _____
g) How to preach _____
h) Is there life after death? A Christian _____
   answer
i) Is there life after death? The spir- _____
   itualist search
j) Life of Christ _____
k) A concordance to Psalms _____
l) John Locke's An essay concerning _____
   human understanding
m) Child psychology _____
n) Validity of knowledge _____
o) The Christian church in China _____

---

a. 296.09
b. 341; 341.69
c. 292.211
d. 266.09519
e. 267.3973
f. 261.8 [18th ed.] 261.6 [16th ed.]
g. 251
h. 236.2 [18th ed.] 237 [16th ed.]
i. 133.9013 [18th ed.] 133.9 [16th ed.] The numbers for
   immortality in 129.6 and 218 would not be in correct
   divisions.
j. 232.901 [18th ed.] 232.9 [16th ed.]
k. 223.202
l. 190, 192, or 153.7 [18th ed.] 152.7 [16th ed.] [192
   preferred]
m. 155.4 [18th ed.] 136.7 [16th ed.]
n. 120
o. 275.1

Regarding m. above, the 17th edition provided an entirely
new psychology schedule.

66. 914-919 may be divided like 940-990 [16th ed.] or you may add area notations to 91 [18th ed.] for the geography of the modern world.

Hence a Geography of Japan would be classed under 915.2.

Where would you classify the following?

a) Travel in Ireland _____
b) The mountains of Europe _____

---

a) 914.15
b) 914.0943 [see note under 09 under 914-919]

67. Biographies may be classed in several ways.

Many libraries class individual biography in B or 92, arranging alphabetically by subject's name.

For example, a biography of Mozart might appear under B or 92, and with all other biographies classed under B or 92 it would be arranged alphabetically by subject, i.e., Mozart. Hence, on the shelf it would appear after a biography of Livingstone but before a biography of Washington.

Collective biography may be classed in 920 arranged by author's name.

Both collective and individual biography, or collective biography only, may be classed in 921-928 divided like the whole classification, e.g., the life of a doctor or doctors: 926.1, the life of a group of baseball players: 927.96357

Go on to the next frame.

68. Or, and this is to be preferred, individual and collective biography may be classed in the subject of greatest relevance with the form division 092.

How would you class the life of a musician or musicians? _____

780.92–780 for music and .92 for biography

(The biography number, 920, would be used only for collective biography too general to be classed with any subject, such as general biographical reference works.)

69.   930 is a period division (a division by time) for ancient history subdivided geographically.

940-990 is modern history divided geographically and subdivided in many instances chronologically.

Many classifiers now prefer to class all of a country's history together, e.g., all of the history of India in 954 rather than ancient in 934 and modern only in 954.

Using the modern practice described in the paragraph above, assign class numbers to the following.

a)   History of India from ancient times to the present

b)   Decline and fall of the Roman empire   _____

c)   Holy Roman Empire 843-1519   _____

d)   France under Napoleon   _____

e)   History of national flags   _____

f)   Great religious leaders, a biographical collection

g)   An atlas of Asia   _____

---

a. 954
b. 937.09
c. 943.02
d. 944.05
e. 929.9
f. 209.2 or 922
g. 912.5

Notice that a number preceded by a zero is usually either a period division or a standard subdivision.

70. Language (from 420 on) and literature (from 820 on) are primarily divided by language, with 410 being used for comparative language and 810 for American literature. These two classes are not divided in exactly the same way, although they illustrate one of the features of the Dewey Decimal Classification, i.e., the use of mnemonic (memory) aids. The same number may be used to express the same subject in many places throughout the classification scheme. For example, the number for English is 2, for German 3, French 4, Italian 5, and so on. Hence, the class number for French literature is 840, for German literature 830. However, it must be understood that while, for example, Italian, is always 5, 5 is by no means always Italian. Grammar is 5, the form division for periodicals is 5, and Asia is 5. As Dewey says, "The purpose (of this memory device) is to give practical aid, not to follow fanciful theory."

Divisions like those under 420 are used elsewhere-- thus a French-English dictionary would be what number? _____

443.2 (the .2 means English)

71. Some libraries, particularly <u>public</u> and <u>school</u> libraries, class fiction in F rather than a DC number.

For libraries which class fiction in DC, it is classed by original language. An English translation of a Russian novel would stand with the Russian original in the number for Russian literature.

Where then, would you classify the following:

a) Kafka's "The trial" translated from the German by W. Muir? _____
b) The novels of Pushkin translated from the Russian _____

---

a) 833
b) 891.7

72. Works about authors are given the same number used for works by those authors. For example, a work about William Shakespeare would receive the same class number as a work by him, i.e., 822.33. This will be discussed in greater detail later in the program.

Go on to the next frame.

73. Literature is divided within language by form--that is, by poetry, drama, fiction, etc.

    Within each language:

    > poetry is 1
    > drama is 2
    > fiction is 3

    American poetry is 811. Write the correct numbers for those listed below.

    a) English poetry   _____
    b) German poetry   _____
    c) English fiction   _____
    d) American fiction   _____
    e) French fiction   _____

---

a. 821; b. 831; c. 823; d. 813; e. 843

74. DC provides for chronological arrangement of authors within form. Some libraries prefer to arrange authors alphabetically within form omitting the period divisions provided in the DC tables.

    English poetry   821

Sub-Arrangement	Chronological	Alphabetical
	Shakespeare (1564-1616)	Drinkwater
	Milton (1608-1674)	Keats
	Keats (1795-1821)	Milton
	Drinkwater (1882-1937)	Shakespeare

Go on to the next frame.

75. Libraries which prefer to keep all works of an author together regardless of form may class him in the form number --8 (Collections). Thus the poetry, plays and novels of an English author would all class in 828 rather than (insert correct numbers):

    _____ for poetry
    _____ for plays
    _____ for novels

821; 822; 823

76. Assign class numbers to the following:

    a) Literary esthetics
    b) Scenario writing
    c) Goethe's Faustus [in the original language, published in 1965]
    d) Dickens' Dombey and son
    e) Spanish-English dictionary
    f) A French text for Americans
    g) Famous quotations
    h) Debating

---

a. 801.93 [18th ed.] 801.9 [16th ed.]
b. 808.066
c. 832 [without period division] or 832.6 [with period division]
d. 823 or 823.8
e. 463.2 [the .2 means English]
f. 448.2421 [18th: "824" from table 4; "21" from table 6]
g. 808.882 [18th ed.] 808.88 [16th ed.]
h. 808.53

77. Some libraries distinguish books of musical scores from books about music by prefixing M to the number within the 780's.

Assign class numbers to the following:

a) History of keyboard instruments   _____
b) A collection of folksongs (scores)   _____
c) A collection of operatic arias (vocal score)   _____
d) A hymnody (without music)   _____
e) History of music   _____
f) Rules for playing mah jong   _____
g) History of Japanese painting   _____
h) History of French painting   _____

---

a. 786.09
b. 784.4 or M784.4
c. 782.15 or M782.15
d. 245
e. 780.9
f. 795.3
g. 759.952
h. 759.4

78. In the 15th ed. DC placed the whole government of a country in 320.9 divided like history. Many libraries continue this practice, reserving 342.3-9 for books concerning the constitution of various countries; and 354.3-9 for books concerning the executive branch of the government of various countries.

For example, a book on the constitution of France would classify at 342.44 and a book on the government of France would classify at 354.44.

Go on to the next frame.

79. The number 301 is a good example of how a form number may be taken for another meaning and two zeros substituted for the original meaning.

301 is now the number for _____.

The number for philosophy of the Social Sciences is
_____.

---

sociology; 300.1

80. History of the social sciences would be _____.

[18th ed.] 300.9 or [16th ed.] 309

81. Assign class numbers to the following:

a) The government of the U.S.
b) History of the British constitution   _____
c) Administration of the FBI   _____
d) Teaching mathematics in the high   _____
    school
e) Labor problems   _____
f) Banking theory   _____
g) Proverbs of Korea   _____
h) Etiquette   _____

---

a. 320.973 or 353
b. 342.4209
c. 353.5
d. 375.51 or 510.7
e. 331
f. 332.1
g. 398.9519
h. 395

82. If you have not already done so, you should now read
     the introduction to DC. Some find the introduction to
     the 16th edition easier to read and understand than that
     to the 18th edition.

     When you have problems with specific numbers you may
     wish to consult Lake Placid Club Education Foundation:

Guide to the Use of Dewey Decimal Classification (1962) under the number in question.

If you are only concerned with DC or other decimal classification systems and not with LC or other mixed notation systems, skip to the subject of book numbers beginning in frame 104.

If you wish to know more about the application of LC (or other mixed notation systems such as Cutter Expansive or the many special subject classification systems) continue to the next frame.

Go on to the next frame.

83. The LC classification tables are issued in multivolume form--frequently one class per volume. Different volumes are issued at different times and are in different editions.

Examine the Outline of the Library of Congress Classification (Washington, 1942).

One class, K (law), has not been completed. Many libraries use book numbers (explained later in the program) to arrange law books by author in the absence of a classification table. Some libraries use Elizabeth M. Moy's A Classification Scheme for Law Books (London: Butterworths, 1968). Moys may be used as either K (with LC) or as 340 (with DC).

Libraries which use those portions of K Law which have been completed by LC, may use for uncompleted portions the letters from the K outline plus a book number. Earlier libraries often used the single letter K plus a book number for all law books.

Some academic and medical libraries rather than using LC's R Medicine, use the National Library of Medicine (NLM) which uses the unused letters of LC, QS-QZ and W.

Go on to the next frame.

84. No index volume for the whole classification has been issued by LC. Each class has its own index and the Library of Congress Subject Headings can also serve as an index since LC class numbers follow most headings in the list. A one-volume index has been published by the Canadian Library Association. A multivolume index has been published by the U.S. Historical Documents Institute (not a government agency).

If you know the class in which the book you are classifying belongs, consult first the index in the volume for that class and then consult the number in the tables.

The individual indexes refer to numbers in other classes for related subjects.

Within each class be sure to use the main index to that class and then the index to additions and changes.

If you have no idea of the main class, even with the help of the Outline, use the LC subject headings or other general index to the classification.

Go on to the next frame.

85. Each class is independent. There are no standard subdivisions to be applied throughout the whole classification.

Some classes have tables of subdivisions to be used as directed in the various divisions of that class.

Examine the H schedule.

The directions are usually from a sequence of numbers to a sequence of numbers and involve mathematical additions, e.g., HQ831-960 divorce by country is divided by table V at the back of the H schedule.

For divorce in Japan add (increment) 107 (the number in table V for Japan) to HQ830 (one less than the first number in the sequence) to yield HQ937, divorce in Japan.

Divorce in France would be _____.

HQ 884   (54 rather than 53 was added because in the main
          schedule we are directed to use the 2d of 4 num-
          bers for general works, and table V gives 4 num-
          bers (53-56) for France, the 2d of which is 54.)

86.   Notice that in this instance A1-A5 may not be used as
       author numbers since they have been given special
       meanings.   (Author numbers are discussed in frames
       175-214.)

       In the case of divorce in Japan, where one number was
       given in table V, A2-A4 and Z6-Z8 have been given
       special meanings and cannot be used as _____
       numbers.

---

author

87.   Sometimes the direction is to divide alphabetically A-Z
       by country, topic or some other basis.   This is some-
       times done with the use of a table given in the sched-
       ule.   Where no other direction is given, use the sys-
       tem used for giving author numbers.

       Under HD5870, labor exchanges, we are told to ar-
       range by industry or trade A-Z using the table on
       pages 78-83.

       The number for an employment agency for servants
       would be _____.

HD 5870.D5

88.   The table directed you from servants to domestic ser-
       vants with the number D5.

       The author number will be added to this so that the
       completed number will have two book numbers.

Notice that LC is arranged numerically until the first decimal, e.g., BV231 would precede BV1645.

After the decimal, arrangement is decimally, e.g., .D49 would precede .D5.

Go on to the next frame.

89. Assign LC class numbers to the titles below:

a) History of Judaism.   _____
b) Koran   _____
c) The Olympian gods.   _____
d) Stories of Christian missions in Korea.   _____
e) History of the YMCA in America.   _____
f) Christ and culture.   _____
g) How to preach.   _____
h) Is there life after death?   A Christian answer.   _____
i) Is there life after death?   The spiritualist search.   _____
j) Life of Christ.   _____
k) A concordance to Psalms.   _____
l) John Locke's An essay concerning human understanding.   _____
m) Child psychology.   _____
n) Validity of knowledge.   _____
o) The Christian church in China.   _____

---

a.   BM155.2 [the "1951-" in the table refers to the publication date of the book, not the period covered; we will assume that you are classifying a new book]
b.   BP100 [this would be the Koran itself, not a book about the Koran]
c.   BL782 or BL795.G6 [depending on the nature of the book; you can not classify exactly from the title alone without an examination of the text]
d.   BV2087 or BV3460 [same as above]
e.   BV1040
f.   BR115.C8 [the C8 represents "Culture" and will bring this book into alphabetic order with other topics]
g.   BV4211.2
h.   BT921.2 [assume that you are classifying a new book

published after 1951]
i. BP573.I5 [the "I5" is in the index but you would not
    know yet how to assign it yourself]
j. BT301.2
k. BS1434 [in LC there are no form numbers to be applied
    at various points; the forms are listed in the schedule
    itself]
l. B1291 [you had five numbers 1290-1294; you are told in
    the table to use 1 for editions with commentaries; if
    this had been a book about Locke's essay, the number
    would have been B1294]
m. BF721
n. BD161
o. BR1285

90. If, in letter o above the book has been about Missions
     in China, the number would have been _____.

BV3415.2

91. As you have observed, LC is a very specific classifi-
     cation, particularly in areas where many books have
     been written. The post 1950 division is supplied in
     Chinese missions and not in China church history be-
     cause more has been written about the former.

     If you feel that you have sufficient practice in LC skip
     to frame 99. If not, continue with the following
     frames.

     Assign LC class numbers to the following titles:

     a) History of India from ancient times
         to the present
     b) Decline and fall of the Roman empire   _____
     c) Holy Roman Empire 843-1519   _____
     d) France under Napoleon   _____
     e) History of national flags
     f) Great religious leaders, a biographical _____
         collection
     g) An atlas of Asia   _____

---

a. DS436
b. DG311
c. DD125
d. DC201
e. JC345
f. BL72
g. G2200

92. In DS436 above, assume that the author is a modern European writer whose name is Aaron. May .A1 be used as the author number? _____

No

93. .A1 is reserved for oriental authors, .A2 for early European. It will be necessary to use what number for Aaron? _____

.A3

94. Examine the outline of the P schedule in the Outline.

Notice that language and literature have been combined in one class but that language has its own sequence of divisions (PA-PM) leaving literature in PN-PZ.

Notice that division is by language. Within language division is by period with individual numbers being given to well known authors in the tables themselves.

Notice, however, that PZ3 and PZ4 are used for fiction. (PZ4 is for authors whose first publication is after 1951.)

Fiction acquired for recreational reading may be placed in these numbers. Fiction acquired for academic purposes is best classed by the original language of the author with the other literature of that language. Many academic libraries do not use PZ3 and PZ4.

Assign LC class numbers to the following titles:

a) Literary esthetics
b) Scenario writing
c) Goethe's Faustus in the original language, published in 1965
d) Dickens' Dombey and son
e) Spanish-English dictionary
f) A French reader for Americans
g) Famous quotations
h) Debating

---

a. PN45
b. PN1997
c. PT1916.A1.1965 [the date is that of publication]
d. PR4559
e. PC4640 [you were directed to divide like PC1073-1673; an Italian-English dictionary is PC1640, therefore a Spanish-English dictionary would be PC4640]
f. PC2115
g. PN6081
h. PN4181

95. Assign LC class numbers to the following titles:

a) History of keyboard instruments
b) A collection of folksongs (scores)
c) A collection of operatic arias (vocal score)
d) A hymnody (without music)
e) History of music
f) Rules for playing mah jong
g) History of Japanese painting
h) History of French painting

---

a. ML549
b. M1627
c. M1502
d. BV310
e. ML160
f. GV1299.M3
g. ND1050
h. ND541 (For explanation, see next frame)

96. In example h above, at ND201-1113 you were instructed to divide by table IV. Table IV gave for France general works the number 341. This means that the 341st number in the sequence 201-1113 is the number to be used. The 341st number is found by adding 341 to one less than the first number in the sequence, i.e., 200. Thus the 341st number in the sequence 201-1113 is 200 plus 341 or ND541.

To illustrate this with a simpler number, the number for America in table IV is 01. A history of American painting would be _____.

ND201

97. ND201 (200 plus 01) is the first number in the 201-1113 sequence; it would not be ND202 (201 plus 01). ND202 is the second number in the sequence (200 plus 02) and would mean the history of _____ painting.

Spanish American

98. Assign LC class numbers to the following titles:

a) The government of the U.S.
b) History of the British constitution _____
c) Administration of the FBI _____
d) Teaching mathematics in the high school _____
e) Labor problems _____
f) Banking theory _____
g) Proverbs of Korea _____
h) Etiquette _____

---

a. JK31 or JK421 [depending on the nature of the book when examined]
b. JN118
c. JK873 or HV8138 [depending, again, on the nature of the book; sometimes despite its great detail there is

-40-

no exact number in LC for a particular work; the
former number would be used for a work concerned
with the internal administration of the FBI, the latter for a book concerned with broader aspects]

d. QA11 or in some libraries LB1645 [the latter is used
    by the U.S. Office of Education Library but not by
    the Library of Congress; other special education li-
    braries may wish to use it also; it places the teach-
    ing of subjects with teaching rather than with the sub-
    ject being taught]

e. HD5306, HD4854, or HD5706 [depending on the sense in
    which "problem" is used in the title]

f. HG1586

g. PN6519.K8 [you will learn how to assign the "8" later]

h. BJ1850 [assuming that this is a modern American work;
    a number given in a table in parentheses is not added
    to one less than the first number in the sequence but
    is the actual last digit of the correct number]

99. A British book on etiquette for men would be
     _____.

BJ1875

100. "(5)" in the table meaning "Social usages for men"
      becomes the final digit in the BJ1870 to 1879 sequence
      rather than being added to one less than the first num-
      ber as in some other tables. Tables are sometimes
      on the page as here, and sometimes elsewhere with
      a footnote on the page.

      Watch for the parentheses as the clue to use the num-
      ber itself rather than adding it to one less than the
      first number.

      Etiquette in London would be _____.

BJ1879.L8

101. If you have taken both the DC and LC sequences of frames you have noticed that generally speaking the same subjects are in the same classes in both systems, but not always. Etiquette, for example, was in 300 (social sciences) in DC but is in B (philosophy-religion) in LC.

If you are to classify in LC it would be wise to memorize the main classes listed below. You will do little, if any, further memorization of LC since the same numbers are not repeated with the same meanings in more than one class.

Knowing the correct class, however, will allow you to consult the correct schedule's index without first having to consult the Outline, the LC Subject Headings, or a general index.

A   General works
B   Philosophy - Religion
C   Auxiliary sciences of history
D   History (except America)
E-F   America
G   Geography - Anthropology
H   Social sciences
     HB-HJ   Economics
     HM-HX   Sociology
J   Political science
L   Education
M   Music
N   Fine arts
P   Language and literature
Q   Science
R   Medicine
S   Agriculture
T   Technology
U-V   Military and naval science
Z   Bibliography and library science

Go on to the next frame.

102. Within many LC numbers you are instructed to arrange topics alphabetically. Within most numbers, even after the alphabetic topic numbers, books are arranged alphabetically by author.

This arrangement is accomplished by the use of book numbers taken from the tables themselves.

Since LC is such a specific classification usually no more than one or two numbers are needed in addition to the author's surname initial.

Most libraries using LC also use LC's tables for book numbers:

After the initial letter S
  for the second letter: a ch e h i m o p t u
          use number: 2 3 4 5   6 7-8 9

After the initial letters Qu
  for the third letter: a e i o r y
          use number: 3 4 5 6 7 9

After other initial consonants
  for second letter: a e i o r u
      use number: 3 4 5 6 7 8

After initial vowels
  for second letter: b d l m n p r s t
      use number: 2 3   4   5 6 7   8

Thus the number for Anderson would be _____.

. A5

103.   Letters not in the tables take the number before;
       thus O after a vowel (using the 4th table) would be 5,
       rather than 6 as it would be following a consonant.

       Assign two numbers using the LC tables for the fol-
       lowing names:

       a) Williams   _____
       b) Swanson   _____
       c) Angione   _____
       d) Noolan   _____
       e) Aowy   _____

-43-

a. .W54
b. .S93
c. .A54
d. .N65
e. .A59

104. Within most subjects in both LC and DC, books are arranged alphabetically by author.

A book number, based on the author, (or other main entry) is added to the class number to make up the call number.

For LC call numbers the book number follows a decimal and may be on the same line or the line below.

For DC call numbers the book number is a second line with no decimal preceding.

With or without a decimal, book numbers are filed decimally, e.g., D49 precedes D5.

Label each of the following numbers as either LC or DC:

E183.8
.M6D3 _____

327.73072
D18s _____

815.08
R425 _____

DA26.T6 _____

QE797.P9M82 _____

564.8
M95m _____

942.004
C94e _____

LC	DC
DC	LC
DC	LC
	DC

105. Tables for assigning book numbers have been developed by C. A. Cutter. A revision has been made by Kate E. Sanborn. They are distributed by the H. R. Huntting Co.

The two tables in most common use are C. A. Cutter's Three-figure Alfabetic-order Table and his Alfabetic-order Table Altered and Fitted with Three Figures by Miss Kate E. Sanborn.

The former is usually referred to as the Cutter table, the latter as the Cutter-Sanborn table. These two tables are different in structure and application in certain parts and must not be confused.

Open your Cutter or Cutter-Sanborn table so that you may examine it as you read the following frames.

The first portion of the tables consists of consonants except S (and except Q, X, Y, and Z in Cutter).

The beginning letters of surnames are arranged alphabetically beside columns of numbers. Two columns of letters use one column of numbers in most editions.

The book number or author number consists of the first letter of the author's last name (or other main entry term) plus the figures beside the spelling which agrees with the spelling of the author's name.

If the author's name falls between two groups of letters within the tables, the figures beside the upper group are used.

The Cutter author number for Raymond Brown would be? _____

The Cutter-Sanborn number would be? _____

[Cutter] B814
[Cutter-Sanborn] B879

Remember that some libraries would use only one or two of the figures rather than all three.

106. The Cutter number for Melville Dewey would be?

_____

The Cutter-Sanborn number? _____

[Cutter] D515
[Cutter-Sanborn] D519

107. The Cutter number for C. A. Cutter would be?

_____

The Cutter-Sanborn? _____

[Cutter] C981
[Cutter-Sanborn] C991

108. The Cutter number for Chang Kwang-chih would be?
_____. (Remember that in Oriental
names the surname is first.)

The Cutter-Sanborn number? _____

[Cutter] C362
[Cutter-Sanborn] C456

109. The Cutter number for Marie Ann Vigée-Lebrun would
be? _____ (Remember to look by first
part of a compound name.)

The Cutter-Sanborn number? _____

[Cutter] V68
[Cutter-Sanborn] V673

110. The Cutter number for Jan Vermeer would be?

_____

The Cutter-Sanborn number? _____

[Cutter] V59
[Cutter-Sanborn] V523

111.   The Cutter number for George Wainwright would be?

_____

The Cutter-Sanborn number?   _____

[Cutter]   W133
[Cutter-Sanborn]   W141

112.   Remember always to use the number beside the upper
spelling when a name falls between two spellings in
the table, even if the lower one "looks" more like the
name.

If you use only Cutter-Sanborn, skip to frame 119.

If you use Cutter, proceed to the next frame.

---

113.   Vowels and S in the Cutter table are after all other
consonants except Q and XYZ.

Book numbers in vowels and S for users of the Cutter table are made differently from other letters.

For names beginning with vowels and S (except Sc)
the first two letters of the author's name are given
as well as the figures from the table.

The Cutter number for Kate E. Sanborn would be

_____.

Sa 54

114.   The number for J. McRee Elrod would be _____.

El 74

Notice that the script letter L (ℓ) is used since the typed lower case L would look like the number one.

115.　For names or words beginning Sc, the first <u>three</u> letters are used.

The number for the periodical School life would be

_____.

The number for Arthur Schopenhauer would be

_____.

Sch 65
Sch 65

116.　It is not likely that you will have two persons or terms with the same Cutter number in the same class. If this should occur, a difference must be made in the numbers. Instructions for this will be given in frames 122ff.

Go on to the next frame.

117.　Although Q, X, Y, are after S in the Cutter table, only one letter is used.

The number for Arthur Thomas Quiller-Couch would be _____.

Q 41

118.　If you are concerned only with the Cutter table and not the Cutter-Sanborn table, skip to frame 121. If you wish to understand both tables, continue to the next frame.

---

119.   Vowels and S in the Cutter-Sanborn table are after
all other consonants.

In the vowel and S section one column of letters cor-
responds to one column of figures, rather than one
column of figures serving two columns of letters as
in consonants.

Care must be taken to always use the figures to the
left of the letters.

The Cutter-Sanborn number for Kate E. Sanborn
would be _____.

S 198

120.   The Cutter-Sanborn number for J. McRee Elrod
would be _____.

The number for the periodical School life would be
_____.

The number for Arthur Schopenhauer would be
_____.

The number for Arthur Thomas Quiller-Couch would
be _____.

E48
S372
S373
Q6

121.   To sum up the major difference between the Cutter
and Cutter-Sanborn tables:

In the Cutter table:

> consonants except S - 1 letter
> vowels and S except Sc - 2 letters
> Sc - 3 letters

In the Cutter-Sanborn table only one letter is used throughout.

Go on to the next frame.

122. Within one class number no two authors (or other terms) may have the same author number.

Some libraries (particularly those using LC) use regularly only one figure from the tables. If a conflict develops a second figure is added (from the table) to the author number of the new author.

Other libraries use only two figures from the table. If a conflict develops the third figure from the table is added to the author number for the new author.

Where three figures are regularly used, conflicts are less likely to develop, but when they do a fourth figure must be added.

The fourth figure is added with reference to the fore-name of the author (or second word if some other entry). This is done in relation to the letter's position in the alphabet.

The following table may be used.

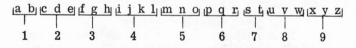

Thus, in a three figure system the author numbers for the Brontë sisters might be: (You can complete the number for Anne.)

	[Cutter]	[Cutter-Sanborn]
Brontë, Charlotte	B789	B869
Brontë, Emily	B7892	B8692
Brontë, Anne	B___	B___

B7891	B8691

123.   As the more prolific writer, Charlotte would probably
have been the first added, and would therefore have
the basic number.   Alphabetic order, then, will not
be exact.

If the fourth figure called for by the table has already
been used for another author, then use the next available higher or lower number to bring the name in as
nearly correct alphabetical order as possible.

At this point rules are not exact and you do that
which works.

Libraries which regularly use only two figures might
have built the Brontë author numbers as follows:

[Cutter]	[Cutter-Sanborn]
B78	B86
B789	B869
B788	B868

(The difficulty with this is that if a person whose
name Brom is later added, a conflict will occur.)

Go on to the next frame.

124.   Assuming that the following author names are all
found within one class number, and that John was
added first, write the Cutter and Cutter-Sanborn numbers for each name.

———————— Churchill, John   ————————
———————— Churchill, Randolph Henry Spencer   ————————
———————— Churchill, Winston   ————————
———————— Churchill, Winston Leonard Spencer ————————

[Cutter]		[Cutter-Sanborn]	
C4	C475	C5	C563
C47	C4756	C56	C5636
C475	C4758	C563	C5638
C476	C4759	C564	C5639

This many conflicts in one class is only likely to occur in
libraries which use F for fiction and B for biography.

125. If the same author has more than one book in the
      same class, they must have different book numbers.

      This difference is made by adding a title letter--the
      first letter of the first word in the title that is not
      an article.

      The following diagram illustrates this and may help
      you understand some of the terms which have been
      used.

      The call numbers shown are for Daniels, Josephus,
      Shirt-sleeve Diplomat.

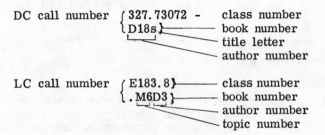

The call number consists of a class number plus a
book number.

The book number consists of an author number plus title letter, date, or any other addition needed to make it unique within the class number.

By now you should recognize that author numbers are also called _____ numbers.

Cutter

126. Back to title letters. Many libraries in DC now add title letters to all books as they are cataloged, assuring correct shelf order if another book by the same author should appear, and making easier the addition of edition numbers (see frame 132).

Title letters are needed more in DC since it is a broader classification and more titles will be found in each of its numbers. LC is such a detailed classification that very few titles appear in any one class number.

In LC title letters are used primarily in fiction.

The book number for Charlotte Brontë's, book, <u>Jane Eyre</u> could be:

Cutter _____

Cutter-Sanborn _____

[Cutter] B789j
[Cutter-Sanborn] B869j

127. For her book, <u>The professor</u>:

Cutter _____

Cutter-Sanborn _____

[Cutter] B789p
[Cutter-Sanborn] B869p

128.   For her Shirley:

    Cutter _____

    Cutter-Sanborn _____

[Cutter] B789s
[Cutter-Sanborn] B869s

129.   For her The spell (assuming that Shirley was cata-
        loged earlier):

    Cutter _____

    Cutter-Sanborn _____

[Cutter] B789sp
[Cutter-Sanborn] B869sp

130.   If the second letter in the title is a vowel, some li-
        braries skip to the next consonant when two title let-
        ters are needed.

        Since there are more consonants than vowels there is
        less possibility of duplication of title letters if only
        consonants are used as second letters.

        Lennox Browne's Voice, song, and speech would be:

    Cutter _____

    Cutter-Sanborn _____

[Cutter] B817v, or B817vo, or B817vc
[Cutter-Sanborn] B882v, or B882vo, or B882vc

131. Book numbers are built as need arises. Those in
      your shelf list for these same titles will not agree
      with the ones given in this program. The situation
      assumed in the program would probably not correspond
      to any one actual collection.

      For example, in an actual situation these two books
      might receive slightly different class numbers, in
      which case they could both have the book number end-
      ing in the single title letter v.

Go on to the next frame.

132. The edition number of a book may be added following
      the title letter.

      Formerly edition numbers were added only when the
      library had more than one edition of a title. Some
      classifiers now feel that, like title letters, edition
      numbers should always be given.

      If an earlier edition is added later by gift, it will be
      difficult to assign a book number if the later edition
      does not have an edition number or date as part of
      its book number.

      This will only be a problem in the larger academic
      library interested in all the editions of a standard
      work; smaller libraries would probably discard the
      earlier edition.

      The book number for the 2d ed. of Wilhelm Brüel's
      Codigo telegraphico Mascotte would be:

      Cutter _____

      Cutter-Sanborn _____

[Cutter] B832c2
[Cutter-Sanborn] B889c2

(If the earlier edition had no title letter, the letter "a" is
used as the title letter for the 2d ed., e.g., B832a2 or
B889a2.)

133. Some titles are frequently republished in different editions, often by different publishers, without edition numbers. The imprint date may be added as a third line of the call number.

The book number for Emily Jane Brontë's Wuthering Heights published in 1924 (the first edition added to the collection) and another edition published in 1940 would be:

	Cutter	Cutter-Sanborn
1924 ed.	_____	_____
1940 ed.	_____	_____
	_____	_____

B7892w	B8692w
B7892w 1940	B8692w 1940

(Some classifiers prefer to use imprint date rather than edition number even where edition number is given, particularly in the sciences. In LC imprint date rather than edition number is always used.)

134. You may have a translation of a work, the original of which is already in the collection. This is indicated in the book number following the title letter by adding the capital initial of the language of the translation and the lower case initial of the translator's surname. LC frequently adds 1 to the basic Cutter plus 3 for English, 4 for French, 5 for German, etc., arranging translations in alphabetical order.

The book number for Charlotte Brontë's Juana Eyre ... tr. al castellano por Leopoldo Terrero, would be:

Cutter _____

Cutter-Sanborn _____

[Cutter] B789jSt
[Cutter-Sanborn] B869jSt

135.   The "S" is for Spanish.

The book number for <u>Jeanne Eyre</u> traduit en francaise par Lesbuzeilles Souvestre would be:

Cutter _____

Cutter-Sanborn _____

[Cutter]   B789jFs
[Cutter-Sanborn]   B869jFs

136.   There are occasions when the Cutter number will be based on subject rather than author.

In LC you are instructed under many numbers to divide alphabetically by topic. In these instances a second Cutter number for author will follow the first based on topic.

For example, a book on Stage hypnotism by Lewis would have the call number BF1156
                                     .57 L585
where the .57 stands for the special topic of hypnotism, i.e., stage hypnotism, L585 is the author number.

Similarly a book on Spies during the Second World War by Halman would be classed under D810
                                     .S6 H161
where .S6 stands for the special topic spies, H161 is the author number.

The Cutter number by subject may completely replace the author number.

Most individual biography and literary criticism are Cuttered by subject.

If the class number indicates that the material is biographical (e.g., DC's -092; LC's BL43 and similar numbers in other schedules) the Cutter number is based on the subject and the first letter of the author's last name is added as title letter.

For autobiography some libraries omit title letter; some use a; some use the first letter of the author's last name as for biography even though the Cutter number is based on the same name.

If the class number does not indicate that the material is biographical (e.g., literary criticism classed with the work being criticised or the author being criticised) an indication is made in the book number.

A capital letter from near the end of the alphabet is used--frequently Z or Y. Some libraries prefer Y because Z when written may resemble the number 2.

This letter is used in much the same way as the language letter for translations.

Assume that John A. T. Robinson's Honest to God has been given the call number 230 R66h. What would be the call number for Oliver F. Clarke's For Christ's Sake, a reply to the Bishop of Woolrich's book Honest to God?

230
R66hYc

137.   For David L. Edwards' The 'Honest to God' debate?

230
R66hYe

138.   Supplements, laboratory manuals, or other accompanying material may be numbered in the same manner in order to have them stand beside the appropriate volume.

For example, a supplement to Schaub's <u>Diagnostic</u> <u>bacteriology</u>, which has the call number $\overline{\text{QR63}}$ might
$$\text{S33}$$
be classed under QR63 so that the two books will
$$\text{S332}$$
appear next to each other on the shelf.

---

139. For a work concerning the whole literary output of an author rather than just one of his works the Y or Z attaches directly to the Cutter number with no title letter intervening.

The book number for a critique of Dickens' novels by Ivor J. C. Brown might be:

Cutter _____

Cutter-Sanborn _____

[Cutter] D555Yb
[Cutter-Sanborn] D548Yb

If "Yb" had already been used, then "Ybr" might be used just as in other title letters.

140. Some libraries prefer to Cutter title letters or use the table in frame 122 for the second letter.

If this method were used the preceding number would have been D555Yb6 or D548Yb6.

The difficulty with this method is that it makes it impossible to use edition numbers.

In LC, title letters are frequently treated this way in classes where title letters are needed.

When title letters are Cuttered, imprint date must be used for editions.

Go on to the next frame.

141.   Assign book numbers to the following, using the table in frame 122 for adding figures to the title letters:

The numbers for Charlotte Brontë's The spell would be:

Cutter   _____

Cutter-Sanborn   _____

B789s6
B869s6

142.   The number for Lennox Browne's Voice, song, and speech would be:

Cutter   _____

Cutter-Sanborn   _____

B817v5
B882v5

143.   Main entries other than authors are Cuttered in the same way as authors.

Book numbers for title main entries usually have no title letters. (LC does not normally use title letters except in fiction.)

Therefore, a book with the main entry "Seminar on the Organization and Handling of Bibliographic Records by Computer" would be assigned the call number in LC (note the absence of title letter in LC)

Z 678.9
S44

where the S44 was the Cutter number for "Seminar.

Similarly the book whose main entry is "Conference on School and Library Relationships" would be assigned the call number

Z718
.C65

where the .C65 was the Cutter number for the first
word of the corporate author. When Cuttering for
Dewey, the title letter would be added.

Go on to the next frame.

144. If a title is in more than one volume, volume number
is added to the call number of each volume, e.g.,
v. 1, v. 2, etc.

If the book mentioned in the previous frame had each
been issued in two volumes, the call numbers for
vol. 2 would have been:

Z678.9		Z718	
.S33	and	.C65	respectively.
v. 2		v. 2	

Go on to the next frame.

145. If more than one copy is added to the collection, copy
numbers are added to copies other than the first,
e.g., c. 2, c. 3, etc.

Both volume and copy numbers are usually the third
line of the call number.

Adding to the call numbers used in the previous frame,
if the books were second copies being added to the
library's collection the call numbers would become:

Z678.9		Z718	
.S33	and	.C65	respectively.
v. 2 c. 2		v. 2 c. 2	

Go on to the next frame.

146. Year is added for most annuals. Year or volume
number may be used for numbered serials, such as
periodicals, in those libraries which classify periodicals.

The Annual Review of Information Service and Technology, volume 4, 1969 would therefore receive the
call number:

Z699
.A1A78
1969

However, the American Journal of Sociology, a periodical, could receive either of the following two call
numbers, depending on whether the library's policy
was to incorporate either the volume or the year in
the call number when classifying periodicals.

HM1   HM1
.A35   or   .A35
v.72   1967

---

147. LC includes special systems for the book numbers of
many prolific authors; DC for a few; see DC's
822.33.

The special classification for works by William Shakespeare is an illustration of this. In DC a biography
on Shakespeare would be classed at 822.33 where the
                                              B
B represented biography.

A text on Hamlet would receive the class number
822.33 while a criticism of Hamlet would be classed
 S7
at 822.33
   S8.

In LC the PR class provides many examples of these
special systems. Shakespeare's tragedies are classed
at PR2763, translations of his works are classed at
PR2775-PR2800 depending on the language of the translation. As in DC, provision is made for classing

separately his individual works.   For example, Hamlet
would be classed at PR2807 and Othello at PR2829.

Go on to the next frame.

148.   The completed call number must be checked against
        the shelf list before using to see that it does not
        duplicate a call number already assigned in libraries
        using DC.

        If the number assigned has already been used for an-
        other book, the new number must be changed by add-
        ing to the Cutter number (for another author) or title
        letter (for another book by the same author) or by
        adding edition number or date (for another edition of
        the same title).

        Some libraries using LC always add imprint year or
        a work mark ("x" or a title letter) to locally assigned
        LC numbers, and do not check the shelf list.

Go on to the next frame.

149.   Now that you have seen how all parts of the call num-
        ber are assigned, you can appreciate the order on the
        shelf which call numbers create.

        1.   Books on the same subject are together.

        2.   Books on related subjects are near each other.

        3.   Books which treat a whole subject in a particular
             way follow those which treat the whole subject
             generally, e.g., a dictionary or history of a sub-
             ject follows a general introduction to the subject.

        4.   Books which treat a part of the subject then fol-
             low in their own groupings.

        5.   Within subject, arrangement is by author.

6. Within author, arrangement is by title.

7. Within title, arrangement is by volume, copy, edition, or date.

8. A translation would stand with its original.

9. A book about another book stands with the book being criticised.

10. A book about the work of an author, philosopher, or artist stands with that person's work.

11. Fiction (F or PZ) and individual biography (B, 92, or CT) in some libraries are not in the subject classed order but instead are given the symbols in parentheses above.

12. Sometimes a symbol is placed above the class number in order to place a book in a special collection, e.g., R or Ref for reference books, j or J for juvenile books, Q (quarto), f (folio) or L (large) for larger books, symbols for branch collections, etc.

Go on to the next frame.

150. There is a whole body of material which is serial in nature, ranging from the daily newspaper through periodicals to monographs issued in numbered series.

Many libraries do not class newspapers and periodicals, but rather arrange them alphabetically by title.

Serials other than newspapers and periodicals which continue in the same form are usually classed to stand together on the shelf.

Examples of such serials would be encyclopedia and other yearbooks and such subject series as Advances in applied microbiology which may or may not be issued yearly.

Series such as Reference shelf, in which each issue has its own author, title, and subject matter may be classed to stand together or each issue may be classed in its own subject.

When classed to stand together, the individual authors, titles, and subjects may still be shown in the catalog by analytics.

For more on analytics see the program Choice of Main and Added Entries, part of the Modern Library Practices Series.

Go on to the next frame.

151.   With the revision of classification schedules or with the growth of collections it is sometimes necessary to reclassify all or portions of the collection.

Sometimes libraries will decide to change from a local to one of the standard classifications or from DC to LC as they anticipate considerable growth.

Reclassification is frequently more costly and time consuming than initial classification. You may find, however, that you must reclassify; for example, the 150 portion of your DC collection, in view of the new table for psychology in 17th ed. DC., or 510 because of the new table for mathematics in the 18th ed.

You may work from the shelf list. If the new number can be assigned from the information contained on the shelf list card--and this is usually possible particularly if the shelf card is a printed unit card with subject headings--note the new number in pencil on the shelf card.

It is best to keep local classification in LC or DC as close to LC printed card practice or H. W. Wilson Company practice as possible. This will allow you to take advantage of classification numbers to be found on printed cards.

If you are concerned with reclassification into LC, go on to the next frame; if not skip to frame 153.

Go on to the next frame.

152.   One method of reclassifying a collection is termed
        'osmosis.' In this context osmosis means the natural
        movement of materials from one classification to an-
        other, with minimum interruption of library service.

        This is achieved by reclassing on the basis of circu-
        lation, allowing patrons, in the course of natural use,
        to select for first attention those items in greatest
        demand.

        While the reference collection might be done as a
        unit, other material in the collection might be re-
        classed using the following procedures:

        1. After being arranged for filing by call number
            (usually) charge cards (the cards by which books
            are checked out) are given to the reclassifiers.

        2. The LC number is copied on the back of the
            charge card and "SAVE" on the front.   The
            charge card is then returned to the circulation
            desk.

            The LC number may be obtained from LC printed
            cards or the LC classification schedules and au-
            thor number scheme.

        3. The shelf list cards corresponding to those charge
            cards are pulled daily.

            (At first, to prevent over-loading the process,
            only printed shelf list cards showing the LC num-
            ber, or post-1950 imprints, or cards not having
            multiple copies or volumes might be pulled.)

        4. After writing the LC number on the back of the
            charge card and returning it to the circulation
            desk, the number may be written on the top of
            the shelf list card.

        5. The shelf list card may now be used as a tem-
            porary card to replace the main entry in the cat-
            alog.

        6. While the book is in circulation the cards may be
            prepared with the new class number.

7. This may be done by covering the old class number on the main entry with Snopake (Litho-Art Products, Inc. 1338 W. Belmont, Chicago, Illinois) or a similar product.

8. The new class number may now be typed in. Various formats have been used:

LD
4711
.R35

LD 4711
.R35

LD4711.
R35

Some even omit the decimal.

9. This main entry card may now be photoduplicated (General Microfilm, 100 Inman Street, Cambridge, Massachusetts) to produce the number of cards needed to provide a full set.

10. The cards of the new set "bump" or replace the old cards in the catalog, saving the time it would require to pull them as an independent operation.

11. When the book is returned at the circulation desk, it goes to be lettered with its new call number, the letterer taking the number from the back of the old charge card.

12. Much time can be saved in retyping the sets of cards if the "checked tracing" method of preparing subject headings is used.

If you are not concerned with this method, skip to frame 153.

13. This method presupposes a divided catalog with all subjects in one file (except perhaps persons as subjects).

14. Subject headings rather than being typed on the cards themselves are typed on guide cards, one for each established subject heading.

Cards for use as guides, 1/2 cm taller than standard cards but otherwise identical to them, and with protective plastic covers, are available on special order from Gaylord (155 Gifford Street, Syracuse, New York).

15. Subject headings are typed on the guide cards using the same forms given in the program <u>Construction and Adaptation of the Unit Card,</u> part of the EMI Modern Library Practices Series.

16. On each <u>subject card</u> the appropriate heading is checked <u>or highlighted</u> in the tracing, and is filed behind the corresponding guide card.

    Thus when a subject heading has been typed once, it need never be typed again.

    A sample subject card follows.

QP
251
N32
1976

Nalbandov, Andrew Vladimir, 1912-
    Reproductive physiology of mammals and birds : the comparative physiology of domestic and laboratory animals and man / A. V. Nalbandov, with a chapter by Brian Cook. — 3d ed. — San Francisco : W. H. Freeman, c1976.

    xv, 334 p. : ill. ; 24 cm. — (A Series of books in agricultural science)

Previously published under title: Reproductive physiology.
Includes bibliographies and index.
ISBN 0-7167-0843-4

1. Reproduction. 2. Physiology, Comparative.   I. Cook, Brian.   II. Title.
[DNLM: 1. Physiology, Comparative.   2. Reproduction.   QT4 N165r]

QP251.N32   1976   599'.01'6   75-25890
                                                                 MARC

Library of Congress   75

---

17. The guide cards may replace the subject authority file.

18. See references should be typed on the taller guide cards rather than on standard cards.

Go on to the next frame.

153. You have now completed the portions of this program that are applicable in most libraries.

    If you are concerned with the application of class

numbers to a classed catalog or shelf list references, procede to the next frame.

If you are not concerned with the classed catalog but are in a special or overseas library, skip to frame 167.

Otherwise you have now completed this program.

---

154.   The shelf list is arranged by call number. Its arrangement is therefore basically a classed one.

The shelf list is not a classed catalog, however. A shelf list has only one card per title; if you looked under a particular number in the shelf list you would not find nearly all the books on that subject; books which contained that subject along with one or two other subjects, books in series kept together, and many others would not be there.

A classed catalog has more than one card per title if needed to represent the subject content of a book.

A classed catalog has an alphabetic subject index to the classification in as many languages as needed.

Go on to the next frame.

155.   Any classification system may be used for a classed catalog, but DC will be used as the example in the following frames.

The book <u>U.S.-French foreign relations</u> would be classed in what number? _____

327.73044

156.   It would have classed catalog cards in that number
       and also in the number _____ .

---

327. 44073

157.   The additional number may be noted at time of classi-
       fication on the verso of the title page in parentheses.
       It would be included in the tracing and typed on a
       classed catalog card.

       Following is a sample main entry for a library which
       uses a classed catalog rather than an alphabetic sub-
       ject catalog.

```
599.016
N165r3   Nalbandov, Andrew Vladimir, 1912-
            Reproductive physiology of mammals and
         birds : the comparative physiology of do-
         mestic and laboratory animals and man /
         A. V. Nalbandov ; with a chapter by Brian
         Cook. - 3d ed. - San Francisco : W. H.
         Freeman, c1976.
            xv, 334 p. : ill. ; 24 cm. - (A Series
         of books in agricultural science)
            1. 599.016.  2. 611.6.  I. Cook, Brian.
         II. Title.              III. Series.
```

Go on to the next frame.

158.   Following are the two classed catalog entries. Some
       libraries type the class numbers in red above the
       call number rather than in parentheses to the right
       as shown.

```
                              (599.016)
599.016
N165r3  Nalbandov, Andrew Vladimir, 1912-
            Reproductive physiology of mammals and
        birds : the comparative physiology of do-
        mestic and laboratory animals and man /
        A. V. Nalbandov ; with a chapter by Brian
        Cook. - 3d ed. - San Francisco : W. H.
        Freeman, c1976.
            xv, 334 p. : ill. ; 24 cm. - (A Series
        of books in agricultural science)
            1. 599.016.  2. 611.6.  I. Cook, Brian.
        II. Title.             III. Series.
```

```
                              (611.6)
599.016
N165r3  Nalbandov, Andrew Vladimir, 1912-
            Reproductive physiology of mammals and
        birds : the comparative physiology of do-
        mestic and laboratory animals and man /
        A. V. Nalbandov ; with a chapter by Brian
        Cook. - 3d ed. - San Francisco : W. H.
        Freeman, c1976.
            xv, 334 p. : ill. ; 24 cm. - (A Series
        of books in agricultural science)
            1. 599.016.  2. 611.6.  I. Cook, Brian.
        II. Title.             III. Series.
```

Go on to the next frame.

159. A textbook in algebra and trigonometry would be
      classed in _____ . It would have the following
      classed entries: _____ and _____ .

512; 512; 514

160.   Here are sample cards.

```
512
B837t    Brenke, William Charles, 1874-
             A text-book on advanced algrebra and trig-
         onomety : with tables / by William Charles
         Brenke. - New York : Century, 1910.
             345 p. ; 23 cm.


             1. 512.   2. 514.   I. Title.
```

```
                                           (512)
512
B837t    Brenke, William Charles, 1874-
             A text-book on advanced algrebra and trig-
         onomety : with tables / by William Charles
         Brenke. - New York : Century, 1910.
             345 p. ; 23 cm.


             1. 512.   2. 514.   I. Title.
```

```
512                                    (514)
B837t    Brenke, William Charles, 1874-
              A text-book on advanced algrebra and trig-
         onomety : with tables / by William Charles
         Brenke. - New York : Century, 1910.
              345 p. ; 23 cm.


         1. 512.  2. 514.  I. Title.
```

Go on to the next frame.

161.   Index cards would be made for each class number
        when it is used as a classed catalog entry for the
        first time.

        Index cards would also be made for the section, divi-
        sion, and class of which it is a part if they have not
        already been made.

        Let us assume that 512 has just been used for the
        first time.   Consulting the DC tables we find that it
        is the last link in the following chain: (You insert
        the correct numbers)

        _____   Pure sciences
        _____   Mathematics
        _____   Algebra

500
510
512

162. Consulting a standard list of subject headings as a guide to terms to be used in the index we find that Science, Mathematics, and Algebra are all suggested terms.

The following index cards would then be typed with the corresponding numbers in the table checked (✔) to show that they have been indexed.

```
┌──────────────────────────────────────────────────────┐
│                                                      │
│     Science                              500         │
│                                                      │
│                                                      │
│                                                      │
│                                                      │
│                                                      │
│                                                      │
└──────────────────────────────────────────────────────┘
```

```
┌──────────────────────────────────────────────────────┐
│                                                      │
│     Mathematics                          510         │
│                                                      │
│                                                      │
│                                                      │
│                                                      │
│                                                      │
│                                                      │
└──────────────────────────────────────────────────────┘
```

How many index cards will be needed for 514? ____

With what copy? _____

_____

_____

one
Trigonometry 514

Only the one will be needed since Science and Mathematics
have already been indexed as the checks in the table would
show.

163.   If not already made, what index cards will be re-
       quired by 327.73044?   List all of them below with
       subject headings and numbers.

       a) _____
       b) _____
       c) _____
       d) _____
       e) _____
       f) _____
       g) _____

a.	Social sciences	300
b.	Political science	320
c.	Foreign relations	327
d.	America - Foreign relations	327.7
e.	U.S. - Foreign relations	327.73
f.	U.S. - Foreign relations - Europe	327.7304
g.	U.S. - Foreign relations - France	327.73044

164.   What additional index cards would be required by
       327.44073?   List below.

       a) _____
       b) _____
       c) _____
       d) _____

---

a.	Europe - Foreign relations	327.4
b.	France - Foreign relations	327.44
c.	France - Foreign relations - America	327.4407
d.	France - Foreign relations - U.S.	327.44073

165.   While this seems a great number of index cards to
       make, in actual practice most books added to the col-
       lection will be in numbers already used for which in-
       dex cards have already been made.

       This system of indexing is known as chain indexing,
       and was developed by S. R. Ranganathan.

       Index cards may be filed in the alphabetic author-
       title catalog or in their own alphabetic file as a part
       of the classed catalog.

       For more information on filing see the program Fil-
       ing in the Library Public Catalog and Shelf List, an-
       other program in the Modern Library Practices Series.

       For more information on the classed catalog see Jesse
       H. Shera and Margaret E. Egan's The Classified Cata-
       log (Chicago: A. L. A., 1956).

Go on to the next frame.

166.　Some libraries which retain their alphabetic subject catalog still put additional classed entries in a public shelf list.

These entries are known as shelf list references and are made in the same manner as classed catalog entries.

For more on shelf list references see W. F. Koenig's 1928 "Prefatory Note" to the LC classification schedule for class P.

Unless you are in a special library or a library outside the United States you have now completed this program. If you are interested in special libraries go on to the next frame.

167.　Special libraries and libraries outside the United States may find that they need more numbers for some subjects than provided by either DC or LC.

LC may be added to by using Cutter numbers following a simple number taken from the LC schedule.

Any number of subtopics could be so arranged under the number in LC for the larger topic.

A U.S. government document depository library might class its documents by using the U.S. Superintendent of Documents classification numbers as Cutter numbers after a simple LC number. The U.S. Dept. of State Bulletin for example might be J83.S1.3: the J83 being taken from LC, the S1.3 being the U.S. Superintendent of Documents number for the publication.

Go on to the next frame.

168.　Special libraries frequently need very detailed numbers in one subject but not so detailed numbers in other subjects.

One way to handle this problem in DC would be to limit the length of the numbers assigned to materials outside of the special subject area e.g., use only up to and including the first decimal place, and for classification numbers in the special subject area use as many numbers as are necessary. In the latter case, if the number becomes too long, an alphabetic letter may be used to represent the main class. For example, the DC number for the repair of radios in a special library in that field, would be 621.384187, which is long and bulky. The library might decide to replace the 621.384 (which is the number for radio and micro-wave transmission) with a single symbol standing for this number, e.g., A. Hence all the books in the library about this subject would come first in the collection and the DC number for the repair of radios would become A187 where A was the symbol used to stand for 621.384.

This is much better than using a special classification worked out for that type of library, because numbers from printed cards may still be adopted.

If a local or special subject classification is used, all classification will have to be done by the library.

Insofar as possible it is best to avoid using DC or LC numbers with meanings other than those in the tables or to add numbers to the system.

Both practices may clash with future expansions and will make the use of centralized cataloging more difficult.

For additional information on the use of special classifications you may like to read either:

a) Mills, J. A modern outline of library classification. London: Chapman and Hall, 1960. Chapter 13 pp. 152-7, "Special classifications."

or

b) Sayers, Berwick. Manual of classification. 4th ed. London; Deutsch, 1967. Chapter 24 pp. 333-46, "The task of classifying a special library."

You have now completed this program, and should be sufficiently familiar with the classification procedures to be able to classify books accurately under the supervision of a professional librarian.

For further information and practice in other areas of library practices you may want to consult the other programs in the Modern Library Practices Series.

- Construction and Adaptation of the Unit Card

- Filing in the Public Catalog and Shelf List

- Choice of Subject Headings

- Choice of Main and Added Entries

DATE DUE